THE ANCIENT
MAYA

by Jenny Fretland VanVoorst

Content Adviser:
Jon Hageman, PhD
Associate Professor of Anthropology
Northeastern Illinois University

COMPASS POINT BOOKS
a capstone imprint

Compass Point Books
1710 Roe Crest Drive
North Mankato, MN 56003
www.capstonepub.com

Managing Editor: Catherine Neitge
Designers: Heidi Thompson and Lori Bye
Media Researcher: Eric Gohl
Library Consultant: Kathleen Baxter
Production Specialist: Laura Manthe

Image Credits

Art Resource, N.Y.: Danielle Gustafson, 19; Bridgeman Art Library: © Look and Learn/Private
Collection, 34; Corbis: Frederic Soltan, 39, Gianni Dagli Orti, 42, National Geographic Society, 23;
Fotolia: Cyril Papot, 41; Getty Images: Angelo Cavalli, 25, De Agostini/A. Dagli Orti/DEA, 7, 28,
National Geographic/H. Tom Hall, 31, *National Geographic*/Peter E. Spier, 4, *National Geographic*/
Roy H. Anderson, 11, *National Geographic*/Terry W. Rutledge, 33, 35, *National Geographic*/Wilbur
E. Garrett, 29; iStockphotos: Benjamin Howell, 15, Francisco Romero, 43, Lucia Busnello, 9;
Newscom: akg-images, 13, akg-images/Werner Forman, 12, 17, EPA/Ulises Rodriguez, 21, Getty
Images/AFP/Luis Acosta, 16, Oronoz/Album, 22; Shutterstock: Ales Liska, 6, alex.makarova,
cover (bottom right), Brandon Bourdages, 40, Christian Wilkinson, 10, lrafael, cover (top right),
Joakim Lloyd Raboff, 36, Kamira, 30, Vadim Petrakov, 18, 26, VojtechVlk, 38, Yummyphotos, 20;
Wikipedia: AndonicO, cover (bottom left), Public Domain, 5, 27

Design Elements: Shutterstock: LeshaBu, MADDRAT, renew studio

Library of Congress Cataloging-in-Publication Data
  VanVoorst, Jennifer, 1972–
The ancient Maya / by Jenny Fretland VanVoorst.
     p. cm.—(Exploring the ancient world)
Includes bibliographical references and index.
 ISBN 978-0-7565-4564-2 (library binding)
 ISBN 978-0-7565-4584-0 (paperback)
 ISBN 978-0-7565-4626-7 (ebook PDF)
 1. Mayas—Juvenile literature. 2. Mayas—Social life and customs—Juvenile literature.
 3. Civilization, Ancient—Juvenile literature. 4. Mexico—Civilization—Juvenile literature.
 5. Central America—Civilization—Juvenile literature. I. Title.
 F1435.V26 2013
 972.81—dc23   2012001966

Editor's Note: Compass Point Books uses new abbreviations to
distinguish time periods. For ancient times, instead of BC, we
use BCE, which means before the common era. BC means before
Christ. Similarly, we use CE, which means in the common era,
instead of AD. The abbreviation AD stands for the Latin phrase
anno Domini, which means in the year of our Lord, referring to Jesus Christ.

Printed in the United States of America in Stevens Point, Wisconsin.
032012   006678WZF12

Table of CONTENTS

Chapter 1

The World of the MAYA

The ball court was a commotion of activity. With hips swinging and elbows jabbing, the players jostled for control of the heavy rubber ball. They moved nimbly, despite the thick protective padding they wore around their waists, elbows, and knees.

They were trying to get the ball through a small ring at the top of the wall without using their hands or feet. And the cost of losing couldn't be higher: Sometimes the losers would be taken prisoner by the winning team, to be used as slaves or possibly killed—sacrificed to appease the gods.

The spectators in the stands cheered as their team gained control of the ball. Times had been tough. There had been drought, and the maize harvest was expected to be poor. But if their team won, they would have victims worthy of sacrifice. With new offerings of blood, they could perhaps persuade the rain god, Chak, to make the rain fall. Perhaps Yum Ka'x, the god of agriculture, would find a way to ensure a good harvest after all.

This was how the world worked for the ancient Maya. Ceremonies, rituals, and even games were used to bridge the gap between the natural and supernatural worlds and to ensure order, harmony, and plenty. The powers of the gods determined the ways in which the Maya adapted to their environment and organized their society. They also influenced how the Maya conducted trade, waged warfare,

The ancient Maya ball game of pok-a-tok (left) was much more than a game. Its outcome was key to relationships with gods, such as Chak (above).

Archaeological work continues on the ruins of Palenque in southern Mexico.

of the north and the rocky highlands to the south. The land of the Maya included parts of present-day southern Mexico, Belize, Guatemala, Honduras, and El Salvador.

The Maya civilization flourished for more than 2,000 years. It was at its peak from about 250 to 900 CE, about 1,750 to 1,100 years ago—a time during which Europe was languishing in what was known as the Dark Ages. While intellectual achievement in Europe was stagnating, an amazing civilization an ocean away was studying the heavens, building spectacular temples and palaces, and creating epic poetry. Some historians say the Maya were the most advanced people in this region of the world at the time.

and dealt with all other aspects of culture and daily life.

This complex and sophisticated civilization had its beginning nearly 4,000 years ago on the Pacific coast of Guatemala. Eventually the people known as the Maya moved east and north, settling in the region now called Mesoamerica. They built their villages in the rain forests of the Yucatán Peninsula. Over time Maya settlements spread beyond the rain forests to the drier lowlands

The time of greatest achievement in the Maya world is known as the Classic Period. During this time the Maya world boasted several hundred cities, some with more than 50,000 citizens. These cities were known for their pyramids, palaces, plazas, and ball courts. Cities such as Tikal, Palenque, Uxmal, and Copán were the seats of vast kingdoms. The people who lived there were farmers and traders, astronomers and priests, warriors and kings. Each had a distinct role to play in Maya society.

Maya cities were made up of several thousand buildings. There were pyramids, temples, palaces, monuments, plazas, roadways, adobe houses, and ball courts. The structures were remarkable examples of engineering, artistry, and just plain hard work. The pyramid is the structure most closely associated with Maya civilization. These buildings were used as tombs as well as a base for temples, giving Maya priests closer proximity to the heavens.

It took thousands of men to build a pyramid with its temple. First the jungle had to be cleared. Then limestone had to be quarried and transported to the building site. Once at the site, the materials needed to be assembled. Some Maya pyramids were more than 200 feet

A procession of musicians from a Maya mural painted in 800

The ancient Maya built numerous cities, many of which can be visited today.

(61 meters) high. The enormous rocks the Maya used weighed many tons, and they had no animals to help them carry the heavy load. All the work was done with human power and without the aid of the wheel. They used tools they crafted out of obsidian, flint, granite, and other stones. They made stone machetes to clear the jungle and stone axes to chop the limestone into blocks. They even made a plumb bob, a heavy stone weight suspended from a string. They used this tool to

make sure the walls of their buildings were perfectly vertical.

After the pyramid was built, artists and craftspeople decorated it with carvings and murals. When the building was finally ready, a dedication ceremony was held. Priests offered gifts to the gods, and musicians played rattles and drums.

Each Maya city had its own king. The larger cities governed the smaller cities around them. The rich and powerful people were noblemen, known as *almehen*. Sometimes their families had ruled the cities for hundreds of years. But most of the Maya were farmers and laborers who worked hard for their king and gave him his way of life.

The king worked too. He was in service to the gods, from whom he drew his power. Through them he was responsible for the livelihood of his people. The Maya believed that if the king didn't perform the proper rituals, the rain wouldn't fall, the sun wouldn't shine, the crops would wither and die, and his people would starve. The king managed an elaborate set of religious practices that kept order and prosperity in the Maya world.

But the prosperity of the Classic Period came to an end

Palenque's King Balam II wearing a jaguar-shaped headdress

around 900 CE. At that time, the Maya began a period of transformation. They continued building pyramids but stopped carving the stone pillars and slabs called stelae. They started abandoning many of their cities. The belief in the divinity of Maya kings was lost, and the Maya began reorganizing under the remaining nobility. By the mid-1500s what was left of the great civilization of the Maya had been crushed by the Spanish conquest.

A stela of a Maya ruler dressed in royal costume was erected in Copán, in western Honduras, in 623.

Stages of Maya Civilization

Period	Duration	Characterized By
Preclassic	1800 BCE–250 CE	Development of writing system, large-scale construction projects
Classic	250–900	Development of great kingdoms, intellectual flourishing
Postclassic	900–1500s	Collapse of kingdoms, kings no longer intervening with the gods on behalf of their people, greater emphasis on commerce

A Maya funeral during the Classic Period in Rio Azul, Guatemala

Chapter 2

A Well-Ordered Universe

The foundation of Maya society was a sense of order and balance. The Maya believed that a sacred force existed in everything, from mountains to plants to people. The key to an orderly society was to use these forces to control and regulate their world.

The Maya believed that Earth was the middle of three

worlds. The watery underworld was the realm of the dead. The upper world, the celestial realm where the gods lived, lay in the sky above the earth.

Gods of the Maya were complex and sometimes contradictory beings. Each one might play several roles, have more than one name, and be depicted in various ways. For example, the central deity of the Maya was Itzamna. In the form of Hunab K'u, he was the creator of the universe, but as Kukulkán, he was the god of writing and learning. Gods could be represented in both human and animal form. When represented in human form, Itzamna was a toothless old man with a large hooked nose, while as Kukulkán he was shown as a serpent covered in feathers.

Ix Chel was the wife of Itzamna. Her

Detail from an altar at the Maya royal city of Copán (left); an urn shaped as the creation god Itzamna (above)

name meant "She of the Rainbow." She was the god of childbirth, weaving, and healing. Still, she seems to have had evil aspects, because in her human form she was depicted as a woman with clawed hands and feet wearing a headdress of snakes. Many of the other gods are descended from Itzamna and Ix Chel. Other gods include Hunahpu, the Venus deity; Yum Cimil, the god of death; Ek Chuah, the patron of merchants; and Yum Ka'x, the god of agriculture—specifically maize. Rain and irrigation were so important to the Maya that the rain god, Chak, took on four forms. Each of the four Chaks was linked to a direction and color. In all, the Maya recognized more than 150 deities.

Earth was the middle realm. The Maya sometimes saw Earth as the back of a turtle swimming in an ancient sea. From Earth grew the sacred tree of life, the ceiba tree. Its leafy crown held up the sky. But although the sacred tree's crown supported the upper world, its roots plunged deep into the watery underworld.

This third realm was Xibalba, a Maya word that roughly translates as "Place of Fear." This was the realm of the dead, ruled by gods of death. The Maya saw Xibalba as a real, physical—but invisible—underground city that could be accessed from Earth via caves. Those who had lived good lives were granted eternal rest in Xibalba, but those who had lived evil lives were condemned to an afterlife of pain and suffering.

Although everything in the Maya world was infused with the sacred force that the Maya called k'ulel, the gods were the most sacred. Maya kings and priests led ceremonies and enacted elaborate rituals to honor the gods and gain their favor. The ceremonies often included giving something to the gods, such as corn, fruit, meat, or incense. The kings and priests also made offerings of jade.

The ancient Maya prized green stones of jade and serpentine more than any other materials.

In Mesoamerica jade was a rare gemstone. It could only be found in the Motagua River valley in what today is Guatemala. Northern Maya traded goods with people living to the south for jade and serpentine. They inscribed these stones with hieroglyphs or carved them into figurines in symbolic shapes to be used in ceremonies. Jade and serpentine items were sometimes offered to the gods or buried with Maya kings when they died.

The mighty ceiba tree

Precious Jade

Jade is a stone that was prized by many ancient cultures. In addition to the ancient Maya, ancient Chinese and Burmese people mined the stone and used it for both practical and sacred ornaments. Jade can be found in a variety of colors, from creamy white to blue and pink, although most artifacts are made of green jade. Bright green jade was the kind mined and prized by the Maya. They associated it with the primal sea, on which the world floated, and with the sky of the celestial world.

Serpentine, sometimes called false jade, was also valuable to the Maya. The stone's name means "serpent rock," referring to its lizard-green color and often scaly texture. The Maya associated serpentine with fertility and carved it into jewelry, tools, and sacred objects.

Jade burial mask of a Maya king

The most important ceremonies required offerings of blood. Because in animals the sacred force was believed to exist in the blood, many Maya religious rituals involved the release of blood through one means or another. The Maya believed that offering sacred blood would bring them the help of the gods.

Sometimes Maya kings offered their own blood to the gods. They pierced their tongues, ears, lips, and other parts of their bodies with thorns or stone knives. Carved stone horizontal beams, ceramic figurines, and pottery show kings, queens, and other nobles performing such acts. These members of the Maya elite had the most to lose if they fell out of favor with the gods.

Other rituals required the blood of sacrifice. Sometimes they killed animals for sacrifice. Other times they killed human beings.

A carved relief features a Maya queen, Lady Xok, and her husband, Shield Jaguar. She pulls a thorny rope through her tongue as a blood sacrifice to the gods.

War was one way the Maya procured victims for sacrifice. The Maya captured their enemies and brought them back to their cities. Sometimes they sacrificed the enemies to the gods during religious ceremonies. Ball games provided victims for sacrifice too.

The Maya played a ball game called pok-a-tok. But it was more than just a game. It was also a sacred ceremony of great ritual importance, and one that often had serious consequences, especially for the losers.

It was very difficult for players to get a pok-a-tok ball through a stone ring.

The game was played in a stone court built for that purpose. The sizes and designs of the courts varied widely. The Great Ball Court at Chichén Itzá was the largest and most spectacular, measuring 545 feet by 225 feet (166 m by 69 m). Many seats surrounded the court, because large numbers of people came to watch the game and bet on its outcome.

In pok-a-tok, two teams, each with one to 11 players, competed to send a heavy, solid rubber ball through a stone ring placed high on the walls of the court. But the players had to score points without using their hands or feet. Only their upper arms, shoulders, waists, hips, and thighs could be used to hit the ball. Players padded their waists, elbows, and knees for protection.

Carvings on the wall of the Great Ball Court at Chichén Itzá show a ball player who has decapitated his losing opponent. This and other evidence suggests that the game was sometimes played to obtain victims for sacrifice.

A ceramic burial figurine of a Maya ball player

Chapter 3

Intellectual
Achievements

Many scholars consider the Maya to have been the most advanced civilization in Mesoamerica. They made unique achievements in literature, mathematics, astronomy, and architecture. One achievement that sets them apart is their system of writing. The Maya were the first in Mesoamerica to develop a written language. Although the Maya spoke more than 25 languages or dialects, they shared a common system of writing. Their written language was made up of pictures and symbols called hieroglyphs. These hieroglyphs, known as glyphs, represented a word, a sound, or a syllable. There were about 700 glyphs. They were written in pairs of vertical columns read left to right and top to bottom in a zigzag pattern.

Only a small percentage of Maya were literate, however. The king, his advisers, some nobles, and scribes knew how to write. Scribes were responsible for writing the stories and history of the Maya. They carved hieroglyphics on stone columns called stelae. They painted them on pottery. They also wrote on deerskin or paper made of fig tree bark, which was folded like an accordion to form a book. The books were called codices.

Maya hieroglyphs appeared in pairs of columns (left). A copy of the *Dresden Codex* (above), named after a German library, is displayed in Guatemala.

Three codices remain today. Because so much of what we know about the Maya comes from the Spanish conquerors, the codices are special because they enable us to learn about the Maya through their own words. They reveal the Maya interest in astronomy and its use in prophecy.

The three codices predict the future based on Maya astronomy and calendars. The longest of the codices is made up of 56 pages painted on both sides. It unfolds to a length of 22 feet (6.7 m). A fourth codex deals with the study of the planet Venus. But scholars believe it is a modern forgery written on ancient paper.

Many scholars believe that the most important book of the Maya is *Popol Vuh*. This poem of nearly 9,000 lines describes the origin of the universe and the creation of the Maya people.

Three codices are known to have survived book burnings by Spanish missionaries in the 1500s.

The Sacred Book

Popol Vuh, the sacred book of the Maya, describes the creation of the world. In it the Hero Twins, Hunahpu and Xbalanque, go to Xibalba, where the gods of the underworld force them to play a series of ball games with life-or-death consequences. Ultimately the twins sacrifice themselves by fire. The death gods grind the twins' bones into powder and throw the powder in a river. But the twins are reborn. They return to Xibalba and trick the death gods into allowing themselves to be killed.

Having defeated death, the Hero Twins are transformed into the main celestial bodies of the Maya—the sun and the planet Venus. Each day they re-enact their descent into Xibalba in the form of the setting sun, and their escape as Venus, the morning or evening star. The story of the Hero Twins is the basis of many Maya customs and beliefs, including the ball game pok-a-tok and the idea of rebirth through sacrifice.

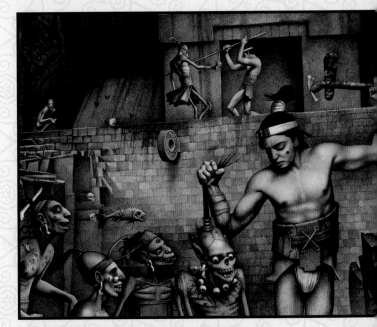

Good triumphs over evil in the the story of the Hero Twins.

The Maya also had a remarkable number system. It consisted of three primary symbols, which could be combined to make any number. A dot represented the number one, a bar was used for five, and a shell represented zero. Some historians believe that the Maya's use of zero was the first example of this concept anywhere in the world.

The Maya used mathematics in their studies of the heavens. They studied the movements of the sun, moon, and stars. They believed that these movements were determined by supernatural forces that, if understood, could be used to bring order to Maya society.

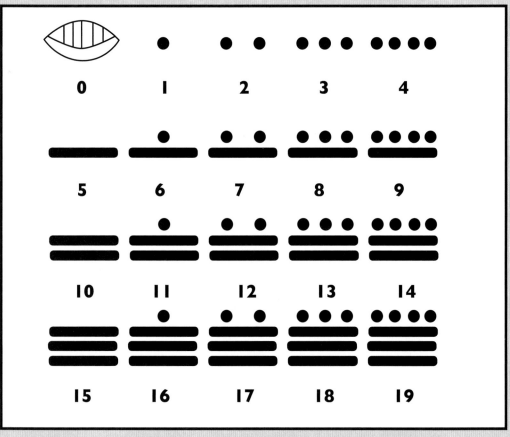

The Maya used a counting system of dots and bars. They used a base number of 20, not 10 like we do.

Detail from a Maya calendar

The Maya did not have telescopes to view the sky. Instead they made a cross out of two sticks and using the naked eye, aligned the center of the cross with distant objects in the sky. This allowed them to accurately note the movements of the planets, sun, and moon as they traveled across the sky.

The Maya made calendars based on their observations. The calendars were used for both practical and mystical purposes. The Maya solar calendar, called the Haab, helped them make predictions about the seasons. It told them when to plant their crops and when to harvest them. It indicated when festivals should be held and what days were lucky or unlucky. It told them which days were sacred, and to which gods. The Haab used a cycle of 365 days, just like our modern calendar.

Other calendars had different purposes and used different numbers of days. The 260-day sacred almanac called the "Count of Days" was thought to determine the destiny of Maya individuals. Each day had a variety of attributes that established the personality and future of a person born on that date. Its influence was believed to be so important that some Maya traditionally named their children after the dates of their births as given in the almanac. This calendar operated without regard to the movements of the sun and moon, simply repeating every 260 days. Some scholars believe that time period was chosen because it is the length of human gestation—the time of development from conception to birth.

The Maya also kept calendars that spanned great lengths of time. The Long Count calendar lasts 5,128 years. Kings used this calendar to locate their reigns in the great cycles of time. December 21, 2012, marks the end of one cycle and the beginning of another.

The significance of Maya calendar cycles can

The placement of Maya structures, including the Pyramid of the Magician in Uxmal, was connected to the cycles of the Maya calendar.

be seen in their architecture. Many Maya temples have features that tie directly to calendar cycles. They may have a certain number of steps based on a calendar. They may have been built with respect to the position of celestial bodies at certain times of the day or year.

For example, the great pyramid at Chichén Itzá was designed with four stairways, each with 91 steps. Add the platform at the top and you have a total of 365 steps—the length of a year. In addition, at the equinoxes—the first day of spring and autumn—the setting sun strikes the edge of the pyramid in such a way that a serpent made of light seems to slither down the steps.

A trick of the light makes it appear as if a serpent is slithering down the steps of the great pyramid, the Temple of Kukulkán, at Chichén Itzá. The body of the serpent joins its carved head at the bottom.

Chapter 4

Daily Life

The class to which people belonged determined their daily lives in Maya society. At the top were the king, priests, scribes, and members of the Maya nobility. Next was the professional class: architects, merchants, warriors, and large landowners. Next were the commoners: craftspeople, small farmers, workers on large estates, laborers, and domestic servants. At the bottom were slaves.

The king and the nobility lived in large stone palaces in the

city. They usually stayed inside their compounds and were only seen by most Maya on public holidays and special events. Noblemen's clothing was usually made of loose cotton that was embroidered and trimmed with feathers. Sometimes they wore robes made of jaguar skins and headdresses made of feathers. Noblewomen dressed more simply. They wore huipiles, loose cotton robes decorated with colorful embroidery.

The Maya used physical appearance to indicate social status. Like the people of all cultures, the ancient Maya had their own ideas about beauty. They thought flat, sloping foreheads were beautiful, and they bound boards to babies' foreheads to flatten them. The Maya knew that an infant's skull is soft and can be shaped easily. The board stayed in place until the skull had hardened into a flattened shape.

Crossed eyes were also considered attractive, so Maya parents trained their children's eyes to cross by tying a small ball to the child's hair so that it dangled atop his or her nose. The child would fix his or her eyes on the ball.

The Bonampak murals (left), painted about 1,200 years ago in Mexico, highlight court life. A Guatemala cave painting (above) reveals the coveted sloping skull.

The Maya ideal of beauty was a large nose and sloping forehead.

Over time the constant inward looking would cause the eyes to permanently cross.

The Maya also thought large noses were beautiful. They wanted their noses to look like birds' beaks. To make their noses look bigger, they sometimes built them up with clay.

Shaped and decorated teeth were another sign of beauty for the ancient Maya. Some people filed their front teeth into sharp points or other shapes. Sometimes they glued pieces of jade or obsidian, a dark volcanic glass, to their teeth. They also pierced their ears, noses, and lips and decorated their bodies with tattoos and paint. Priests painted themselves blue, the color the Maya associated with sacrifice. Warriors painted themselves black and red, while their captives were painted with black and white stripes.

Because of the work of scribes, artists, and skilled craftspeople, we know about the lives of the kings and nobility. But we know very little about ordinary members of Maya society.

Commoners made up the bulk of Maya society, and it was their labor that made the lives of the nobility possible. Farmers were required to

Everyday life in a Maya village

give two-thirds of their harvests to the upper class. The primary crop of the Maya was maize. They also grew beans, squash, cassava, and chili peppers, as well as pineapples, papayas, cacao, and a variety of herbs.

The Maya used a farming method called slash-and-burn. During the dry season, they cut down all the plants in one area of the rain forest. They let the plants dry and then burned them, creating ash, which they mixed with the soil. The ash made the soil richer, and the Maya farmed the new plot until it was no longer fertile. Then they started the process over in another part of the rain forest. The Maya also drained swamps and dug irrigation ditches to create more cropland. They built terraces on hillsides to make the land level and planted crops there too.

Maya farmers lived in small villages near their fields. They tied poles together to make frameworks for their houses, and they covered the roofs with thatch made from palm leaves. Everyone helped with the work. The men and boys cleared and maintained the fields for farming and planted the seeds. They also hunted rabbit, deer, peccary, tapir, monkeys, and birds. Coastal Maya fished and caught shellfish and snails.

Maya women were responsible for the household and the children. They ground maize into flour on a stone called a metate and used the flour to create dough. They formed the dough into tamales, a staple of the Maya diet.

In addition to cooking, the women made and painted clay jars and pots and made the fabric used for clothing. They wove strong and beautiful cloth into which they incorporated ancient designs and symbols. They also wove baskets and mats out of plant fibers.

Slaves were the poorest people and had very difficult lives. Many hauled stones from quarries for

A Maya weaver's water lily and decorated mat indicate that she is royalty.

building projects. They also worked in their owners' houses. When the owners died, slaves were often killed and buried with their owners. People believed that their slaves could serve them in the afterlife.

Some people were born into slavery. Others became slaves when they broke the law or were taken prisoner in war. People bought and sold—or traded—slaves at the market.

The market was an important part of Maya society. As Maya

Maya slaves hauled huge statues and limestone blocks through the jungle.

villages grew, farmers and craftspeople began to trade the things they had made. Maya traders had no horses or wheeled carts to carry their goods, so they had to carry everything themselves. They used a sling called a tumpline to carry their items to market. A tumpline was a strap across the carrier's forehead or chest used to help support the weight of bundles or pots.

The Maya traded fruits and vegetables, salt, animal furs, feathers, and cotton. They also traded things they made, such as jade jewelry, stone tools, cloth, pottery, and bark paper. They used small jade beads and cacao beans as money. These beans, which form the basis of chocolate, were so valuable that only wealthy people had enough cacao beans to make chocolate. The Maya drank

The Maya carried pots and other items on wood frames.

the chocolate in liquid form. Liquid chocolate was believed to contain great powers.

Chapter 5

Decline and Fall

Beginning around 800 CE, many Maya began leaving the cities. They stopped building temples and palaces, and they no longer created monuments to honor their gods.

Nobody knows why Maya civilization collapsed, but historians have proposed a number of theories. Some believe that war or disease caused the Maya to leave their homes in some cities. Others think drought caused a massive crop failure and famine. Many Maya may have moved out of the cities to farm new areas or find food elsewhere. Others believe that a decline in trade caused the Maya to abandon their cities. Another theory is that a natural disaster caused widespread destruction, and the Maya chose to move rather than rebuild. The Maya in each city may have had a different reason for leaving.

By 900 many cities in the southern Maya region, such as Tikal, had been abandoned. While no one knows why the people left, it's clear that many traveled north. Cities in the north thrived and grew. After 900 a few cities in the Yucatán, such as Chichén Itzá and Uxmal, became very large.

The Postclassic Period, which began at that time, was characterized by increased warfare, commerce, and communication with other parts of Mesoamerica. There were frequent changes of rulers, and the political instability often led to civil unrest. By 1221 Chichén Itzá and Uxmal were abandoned, but at about the same time, the city of Mayapan was founded. Mayapan became a major market city, with new items such as copper bells from western Mexico being traded in addition to salt, cotton, honey, pottery, slaves, and stone tools. Mayapan was abandoned in the 1440s after several noble families fought with one another for control of the city. After Mayapan fell, small territories were controlled by strong families. Eventually plants and soil covered the once-bustling cities. The great temples were forgotten.

Tikal, in northern Guatemala, was the largest Maya urban center.

Prominent Maya cities

City	Peak Population	Known For
Tikal	70,000	The Great Plaza
Calakmul	60,000	Structure 2, stelae
Chichén Itzá	50,000	Temple of Kukulkán
Uxmal	25,000	Pyramid of the Magician
Copán	25,000	Hieroglyphic Stairway glyphs
Palenque	7,000	Temple of the Inscriptions

Glyphs from the Copán ruins in western Honduras

Muralist Diego Rivera's depiction of the arrival of conquistador Hernán Cortés

Although the reason for the beginning of the end is in dispute, there is no question as to what dealt the final blow. In the early 1500s Spanish soldiers came to the Americas. They came to explore the land and exploit its natural resources of gold and other riches. They also wanted to spread the Christian religion around the world. The Spanish soldiers were called conquistadors, which means "conquerors" in Spanish.

When the conquistadors reached the land of the Maya, the Spanish fought to gain control of the land. They destroyed many Maya villages and made slaves of the people. They killed many Maya with their guns. They killed even more with the diseases they carried. Epidemics of smallpox, measles, and typhus broke out among the Maya. The Maya and other groups in this region had never been exposed to these European diseases. They had no way to fight

First Encounter

The first known contact between Europeans and the Maya happened in 1502. Christopher Columbus, returning to the Americas on his fourth and final voyage, encountered Maya traders traveling by canoe off the coast of what today is Honduras. Columbus wrote about the experience in his journal. He described coming upon a very long, wide dugout canoe paddled by 25 people. The canoe was full of Maya trade goods such as copper hatchets, wooden swords edged with flint, and embroidered textiles. It also carried cacao beans and a beverage similar to modern beer. Columbus was impressed with the civilization these boats represented, but instead of investigating further, he chose to continue on in search of a passage to the lands of spices—India.

Christopher Columbus

them, and thousands of people died.

The Maya fought the conquistadors for a long time, but in the end they were no match for the Spanish, with their horses and guns. After the Spanish gained control of the land, they tried to erase the Maya culture. They destroyed sacred objects and banned the Maya religion. They burned Maya books. As a result, we know very little about what caused the Maya to abandon their cities hundreds of years earlier.

By 1546 the Spanish ruled most of Mexico and Central America. The establishment of the Spanish capital city of Mérida in 1542 heralded the beginning of the end of independent Maya civilization in Mexico. In 1697 the last independent Maya city in Guatemala was conquered.

Since that time the Maya people have struggled for their rights and freedom. Even after the countries of Mesoamerica declared independence

from Spain, many Maya were still mistreated. In many places Maya were killed or forced to leave their land.

Today there are millions of the descendants of the ancient Maya living in Guatemala, Mexico, Honduras, El Salvador, and Belize. In Guatemala more than half of the people are Maya or mestizo. Mestizos have both Spanish and Maya ancestries and speak a mixture of Spanish and the Maya language. The Maya of today have not fully

A Mérida monument to Mexico's long history

Hidden Cities

The conquering Spanish did not know about the many great structures hidden from view. After falling into decline in the 1200s, many of the major Maya urban centers were abandoned, to be swallowed up by the jungle. They remained undiscovered for centuries. But stories of the vine-covered cities circulated among the Spanish, and in 1839 American explorer John Lloyd Stephens set out to uncover the truth.

The Maya city of Copán was the first to be revealed. Stephens bought the site in Honduras from a chieftain for $50 (the equivalent of about $1,200 today). He and Frederick Catherwood, an English architect and artist, worked on excavating, illustrating, and understanding the site. Eventually more than 60 sites of ruined Maya cities were discovered.

Frederick Catherwood's painting of the ruins of Tulum

A young mother sells traditional textiles in Santa Catarina Polopo, a Maya village in Guatemala.

embraced the western, Christianized culture that the Spanish imposed on them. Many still speak Maya languages and retain many of the beliefs and practices of their ancestors. Their religious ceremonies are a blend of Christian and ancient Maya traditions.

Many of today's Maya are farmers, working the land in much the same way their ancestors did. They use ancient techniques of farming, building, and weaving. Maize remains a staple of the Maya diet and is grown much as it was centuries ago.

The world of the ancient Maya is no more, but its artifacts, architecture, and literature offer a lasting legacy of this great civilization.

Timeline

3114 BCE	The world is created August 13, according to the Maya Long Count calendar
2000 BCE	Maya civilization begins to develop
700 BCE	Writing is developed in Mesoamerica
400 BCE	The earliest known stone solar calendars are used by the Maya
300 BCE	The Maya create a society ruled by kings and nobles
250 CE	The Classic Period begins
500	Tikal becomes a major Maya city
600	The city of Palenque flourishes
700	Temple of the Inscriptions is built at Palenque
738	Copán is conquered by Quiriguá, a rival city, and its king captured
800	Southern cities begin to go into decline, and many are abandoned
869	Construction in Tikal stops, marking the beginning of the city's decline
899	Tikal is abandoned
900	The Classic Period ends with the collapse of most southern lowland cities; Maya cities in the Yucatán grow and thrive
1000	The Maya begin to abandon the northern cities; the *Dresden Codex* is written at Chichén Itzá
1221	Chichén Itzá and Uxmal are abandoned; Mayapan is founded
1502	Christopher Columbus encounters Maya traders off the coast of what now is Honduras
1517	The conquistador Hernandez de Cordoba arrives on the shores of the Yucatán
1524	The conquistador Hernán Cortés encounters the Maya
1542	The Spanish establish their capital city at Mérida on the Yucatán Peninsula
1550	*Popol Vuh* is written
1839	Copán is unearthed from the Honduran jungle by John Lloyd Stephens and Frederick Catherwood

Glossary

almanac—book that contains information on the weather and stars for a particular year

cassava—root that yields an edible starch

codices (singular: codex)—ancient manuscripts made of bark paper or animal skin

deity—god or goddess

equinoxes—two times each year when the sun crosses the equator, and day and night are of about equal length

gestation—development of a fetus in preparation for birth

glyph—written symbol that conveys information

hieroglyphics—system of writing in which pictures or symbols represent words or sounds

maize—corn; the Maya's most important food source

Mesoamerica—region in Central America where native cultures flourished before the Spanish colonization of the Americas in the 16th and 17th centuries

mestizo—person of mixed European and Native American ancestry

metate—large stone on which corn kernels are ground and rolled into a dough

peccary—hoofed mammal related to the pig

primal—earliest; existing before other things

prophecy—prediction of something

stelae (singular: stela)—freestanding stone pillars or slabs that have been inscribed to commemorate an event

tapir—large animal related to the horse and rhinoceros

Select Bibliography

Ackroyd, Peter. *Cities of Blood.* New York: DK Publishing, 2004.

Baudez, Claude, and Sydney Picasso. *Lost Cities of the Maya.*
New York: Harry N. Abrams, 1992.

Cecil, Jessica. *The Fall of the Mayan Civilisation.* BBC: Ancient History
in Depth. 17 Feb. 2011. 3 May 2012. www.bbc.co.uk/history/ancient/cultures/
maya_01.shtml

Coe, Michael D. *The Maya, 8th edition.* New York: Thames & Hudson, 2011.

Foster, Lynn V. *Handbook to Life in the Ancient Maya World.*
Oxford: Oxford University Press, 2005.

Martin, Simon, and Nikolai Grube. *Chronicle of the Maya Kings and Queens:
Deciphering the Dynasties of the Ancient Maya.* London: Thames & Hudson, 2008.

Schele, Linda, and Peter Mathews. *The Code of Kings: The Language of Seven
Sacred Maya Temples and Tombs.* New York: Scribner, 1998.

Sharer, Robert J. *Daily Life in Maya Civilization, 2nd edition.*
Westport, Conn.: Greenwood Press, 2009.

Stuart, Gene S., and George E. Stuart. *Lost Kingdoms of the Maya.*
Washington, D.C.: National Geographic Society, 1993.

Than, Ker. "Maya Mystery Solved by 'Important' Volcanic Discovery?" *National
Geographic.* 18 April 2011. 3 May 2012. http://news.nationalgeographic.com/
news/2011/04/110414-maya-volcanoes-eruptions-ash-tikal-science-volcanic/

Further Reading

Braman, Arlette N. *The Maya: Activities and Crafts from a Mysterious Land.* Hoboken, N.J.: J. Wiley, 2004.

Harris, Nathaniel. *National Geographic Investigates Ancient Maya: Archaeology Unlocks the Secrets of the Maya's Past.* Washington, D.C.: National Geographic, 2008.

Kirkpatrick, Naida. *The Maya.* Chicago: Heinemann Library, 2003.

Kops, Deborah. *Palenque.* Minneapolis: Twenty-First Century Books, 2008.

Maloy, Jackie. *The Ancient Maya.* New York: Children's Press, 2010.

Matthews, Rupert. *You Wouldn't Want to Be a Mayan Soothsayer! Fortunes You'd Rather Not Tell.* New York: Franklin Watts, 2008.

On the Web

Use FactHound to find Internet sites related to this book. All of the sites on FactHound have been researched by our staff.

Here's all you do:

Visit www.facthound.com

Type in this code: 9780756545642

Titles in this Series:

The Byzantine Empire
Ancient China
Ancient Egypt
Ancient Greece
The Ancient Maya
Mesopotamia

Index

About the Author

Jenny Fretland VanVoorst is a writer and editor of books for young people. She enjoys learning about history, from the rise of the ancient Egyptians to the fall of the Soviet Union. When she's not reading and writing, VanVoorst enjoys kayaking, playing the harmonica, and watching wildlife. She lives in Minneapolis, Minnesota, with her husband, Brian, and their two pets.